# Hip Hip Hooray!!

By Grandma G

Illustrated by Patricia Boyer

Designed by Andy Sewell

For Lewis and Mayra Young

*(Da and Ma)*

In Memory Of

**Draeven Blaze Young**

Forever In Our Hearts

*October 17, 2013 - January 20, 2015*

The excited chant filled the heavens.

"Draeven Blaze Young!
Draeven Blaze Young!
Hip Hip Hooray!
It's Draeven Blaze Young!
Draeven Blaze Young!
Hip Hip Hooray!"

"OK, Angel Boys, move back, move back!

Let me through.

Let me welcome this Little Man."

All the Angel Boys gladly sort-of parted
to make a squiggly, sort-of path.

Draeven Blaze Young,
the newest arrival to heaven's playground,
looked up with a Draeven twinkle in his eyes
and a Draeven grin on his face.

And he waddle–toddled as fast as he could,
squealing with his little mom-taught squeal,
(just like when his mom chased him)
right up to the Big Daa.

Looking up into the warm, loving
eyes of the Big Daa, Draeven
immediately lifted his little arms.

Quickly realizing what he had
forgotten, he circled his little belly
with a signing-please and
touched his little chin with
a signing-thank you.

Big Daa threw His head back, let out a happy laugh,
and instantly scooped the Little Man up
and wrapped him tightly in His arms of love.

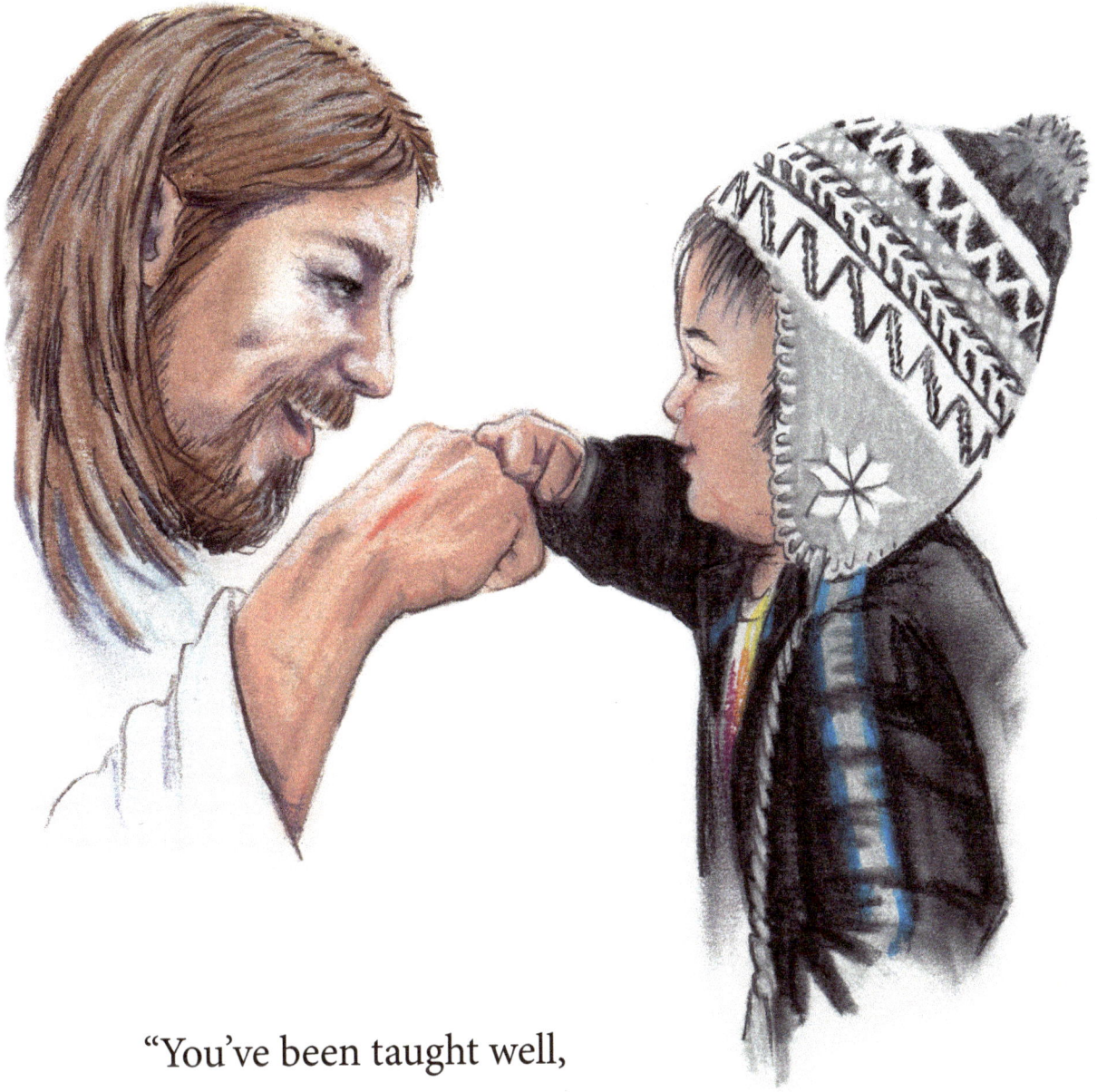

"You've been taught well,
Draeven Blaze Young!
Hey! I watched your Da teach you this!
Give me knuckles!"

And with his little grin, Draeven fist-bumped his Big Daa.

Draeven started squirming, and knowing exactly what that meant,
Big Daa set him down.

"Hey, Little Man! I want to see one more thing your Da
taught you before the Angel Boys give us the tour.
Oh! By the way, when you were little you were called
an Angel Baby. Well, now you are an official Angel Boy!
OK, let me see this!" And Big Daa boomed,

"IT'S
GOOOOOOD!"

Draeven lifted
both arms in the air,
a little ref announcing
a touchdown.

Big Daa laughed and laughed.

"OK, Angel Boys, give me and our newest Angel Boy the tour!
Make it good!! Let's go!"

Draeven grabbed his
Big Daa's finger
and they followed the
Angel Boys on their tour
of the playground.

Knowing the Angel Boys
were leading them
to one of their favorites,
Big Daa whispered,

"Hey, Draeven!

You are going to like this!"

And like it he did! It was a room with nothing but drawers and cupboards. Draeven could open any drawer he wanted or any cupboard he wanted. And he could take anything he wanted. It was all OK.

**Draeven was in heaven!!**

Big Daa laughed heartily as He watched Draeven's delight.

"We'll come back later, Little Man!
Let's see what else they have to show us."

The Angel Boys surrounded Draeven and rushed him into the next room. They could hardly wait to show him! It was a room filled with fruit snacks of every kind.

Draeven ran up and pointed to the first box he found, and several Angel Boys grabbed a package from the box, opened it, and handed the entire package to him.

Draeven
was
in
heaven!!

Next was a room filled with fans and remotes. Lots of Angel Boys grabbed remotes to give to Draeven. They all wanted him to take theirs first. Draeven took one and started pushing buttons. Then he looked up and pointed when he found which fan was turning.

**Draeven was indeed in heaven!!**

Once again, Big Daa
scooped Draeven up.
Draeven babbled softly.

Big Daa understood.

Draeven was looking for his
Da and Ma. The Angel Boys
seemed to understand and
let Big Daa have time with
their new friend.

Big Daa told Draeven
the way it was.

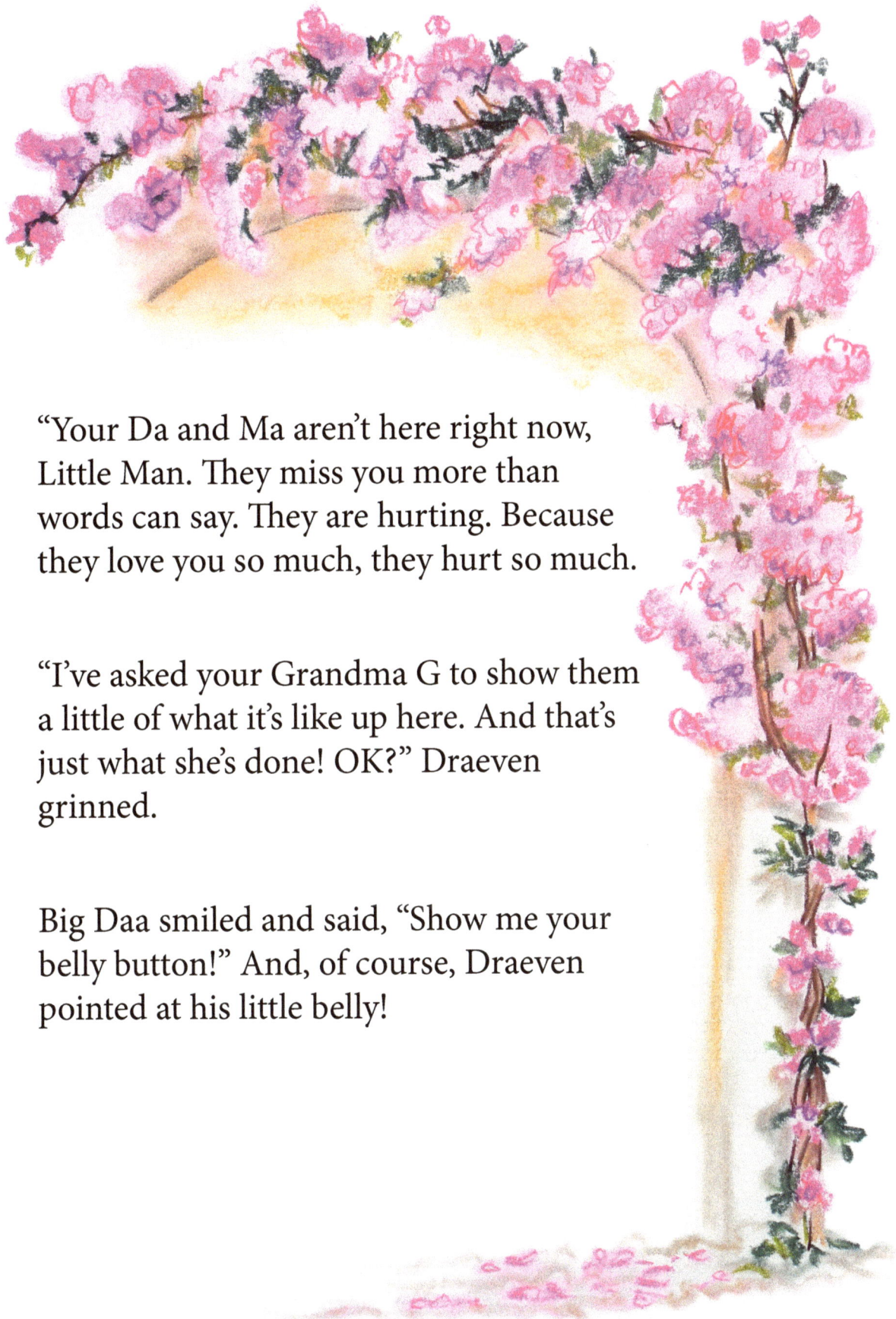

"Your Da and Ma aren't here right now, Little Man. They miss you more than words can say. They are hurting. Because they love you so much, they hurt so much.

"I've asked your Grandma G to show them a little of what it's like up here. And that's just what she's done! OK?" Draeven grinned.

Big Daa smiled and said, "Show me your belly button!" And, of course, Draeven pointed at his little belly!

"OK, Angel Boys, what's next on the tour?"
The Angel Boys grabbed Draeven's little
hands and pulled him along. Big Daa trailed
behind, a big smile on His face.

Next on the tour, Draeven was led to a big
field. The Angel Boys were all pointing and
telling Draeven, "Look! Look at all the perros
and gatos!"

Draeven could pet or chase any of the dogs
and cats and they all welcomed him. He could
even pull their tails and they didn't mind!

And everyone here spoke Spanish-English, just
like Draeven!

**Draeven was in heaven!!**

(perros)

(gatos)

What a place!

There were fields with
footballs, soccer balls,
basketballs and
basketball hoops.

There were rooms
with trucks and cars.

There were rooms with
buttons to push
and switches to switch
and knobs to turn.

There were rooms with pools of water to splash in.

There were forests

with moose

and deer

and birds.

And there was even a storybook room!

**Draeven
was
in
heaven!!**

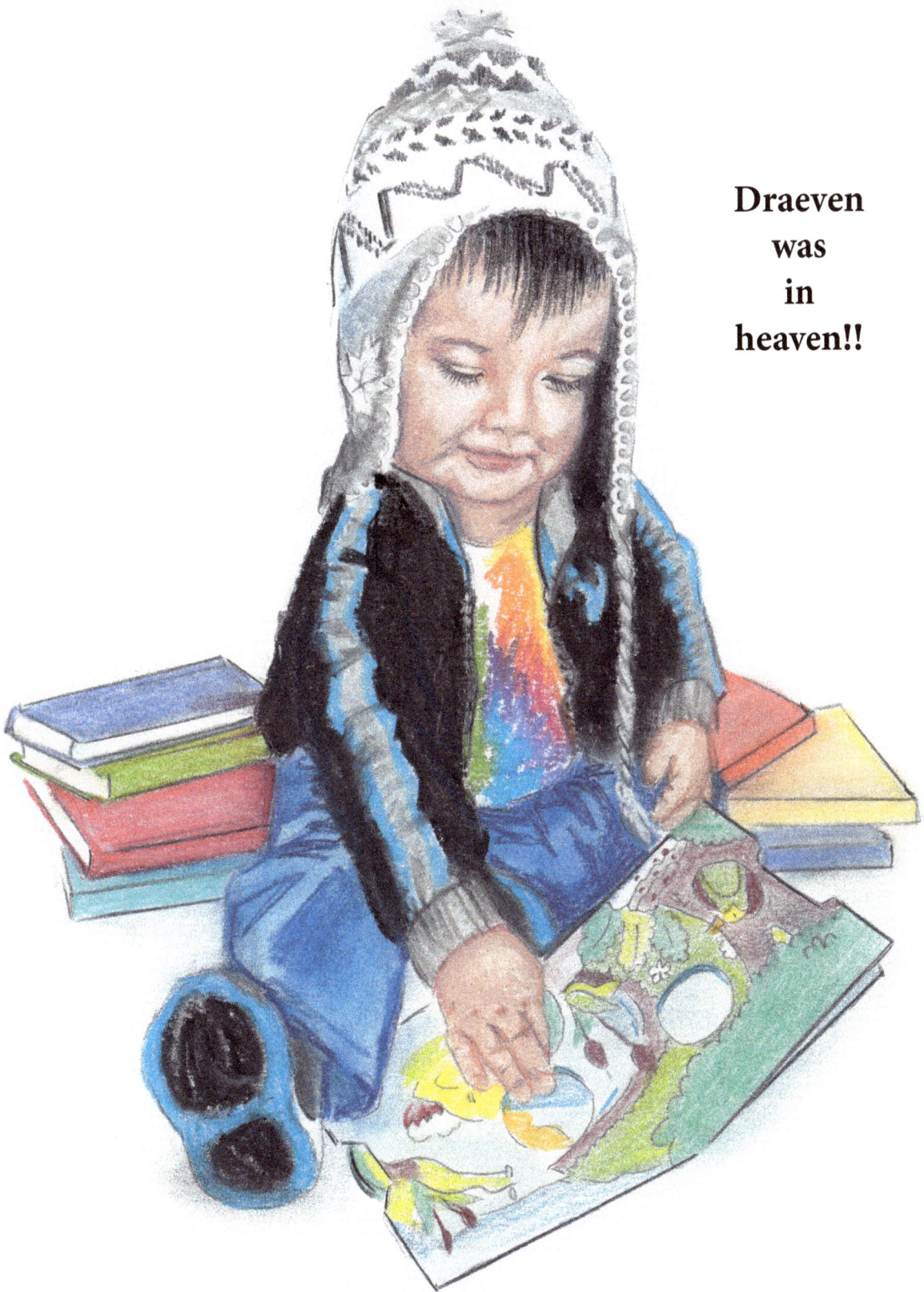

The Big Daa was always
with Draeven.

He held his hand
before Draeven knew
he needed his hand held.

He hugged him
before Draeven knew
he needed a hug.

He lifted him
when Draeven
wanted up.

He let him rest when he wanted to rest.

He even let him pick out a chupón if he wanted a chupón!

*(chupón)*

He let him play when he wanted to play.

Big Daa talked to Draeven often
and Draeven understood.

He told Draeven how He
had always been with him,
watching over him
and taking care
of him.

He talked to him
often about his
Da and Ma.

He told Draeven He was with his Da and Ma, even when they couldn't feel Him or see Him.

He told Draeven He was watching over his Da and Ma and taking care of them and helping them through this time of pain.

Draeven knew what the Big Daa said was true, and he was happy.

And this is what the Big Daa also told Draeven! He whispered it in Draeven's little ear.

"Draeven, your Da and Ma will be here with you some day. And guess what? You'll be together again!

"And you'll get to give them the tour and tell them all about it yourself."

Once again, the Angel Boys' excited chant filled the heavens. This time the newest little Angel Boy's babbling voice joined right in.

"Hip Hip Hooray!

It's Draeven Blaze Young!

Hip Hip Hooray!

Hip Hip Hooray!"

**Draeven is in heaven!!**

# Many Thanks

To Patricia Boyer and Andy Sewell who both know the heartache of losing children.

Pat, thank you for helping us keep Draeven's memory alive through these priceless illustrations.

Andy, thank you for so willingly giving your encouragement, inspiration, ideas, and design skill.

Because of both of you, I know each page is crafted with love and understanding—love for your own children, and understanding of the pain that comes with the untimely separation from a beloved child.

Thank you, Pat and Andy, for sharing with me the hope in your hearts. I look forward to our tour of heaven's playground. And I look forward to the day when together we will laugh and play with these children whom we love so deeply.

Gina Young
(Grandma G)

Pat Boyer: pbloveart@yahoo.com
Andy Sewell: www.finewatercolors.com
Gina Young: sam.gina@gmail.com

www.ingramcontent.com/pod-product-compliance
Lightning Source LLC
Chambersburg PA
CBHW040257100426
42811CB00011B/1290